S0-CAV-772

France
A Photographic Journey

France

A Photographic Journey

Emma Howard

BARNES & NOBLE
NEW YORK

This 2007 edition published by Barnes & Noble, Inc. by arrangement with
Compendium Publishing Limited, First Floor, 43 Frith Street, London W1D 4SA.

Editor: Don Gulbrandsen
Design: Danny Gillespie/Compendium Design
Maps: Mark Franklin

Photo credits: Unless specified below, all photographs for this book were supplied by Jo St. Mart.
Hugh Alexander: 1, 8, 13, 14, 15, 25B, 27, 29, 34T&B, 36B
Getty Images: 2–3 (Camille Moirenc/hemis.fr), 22–23 (International Stock Photography/Taxi), 39 (Arnaud Chicurel/hemis.fr), 58–59 (Digital Vision), 82–83 (Tony Gervis/Robert Harding World Imagery), 90–91 (Simeone Huber), 102–103 (Ian Shaw/Stone), 120 (National Geographic), 156–157 (Sami Sarkis)
Corbis: 30 (Louie Psihoyos), 38 (Patrice Latron), 46 (Richard Klune), 50 (Jose Fuste Raga), 51 (B/Roger Ressmeyer), 54 (Tibor Bognar), 55 (Steven Vidler/Eurasia Press), 60 (Steven Vidler/Eurasia Press), 61 (Christophe Boisvieux), 62–63 (Richard Klune), 64–65 (Bruno Barbier/Robert Harding World Imagery), 66 (T/Patrice Latron; B/Eleanor Bentall), 67 (Giraud Philippe/Corbis Sygma), 68–69 (Archivo Iconografico, S.A.), 70 (Douglas Pearson), 71 (Forestier Yves/Corbis Sygma), 72–73 (Ellen Rooney/Robert Harding World Imagery), 74 (Tony Craddock/zefa), 76 (Douglas Pearson), 79 (Michael Busselle), 84 (Eberhard Streichan/zefa), 85 (T/Doug Pearson/JAI; B/Michael Busselle), 88 (Richard Klune), 94 (Ludovic Maisant), 95 (Steven Vidler), 98 (Sylvain Grandadam/Robert Harding World Imagery), 100–101 (Jose Fuste Raga), 104–105 (Jacques Pavlovsky/Sygma), 106 (T/Arthur Thévenart; B/Lee Snider/Photo Images), 107 (Geoffrey Taunton; Cordaiy Photo Library Ltd), 110 (Steven Vidler/Eurasia Press), 111 (James Andanson/Sygma), 114 (Christophe Boisvieux), 119 (Michael Busselle/Robert Harding World Imagery), 128 (Owen Franken), 131 (Pascal Deloche/Godong), 132 (Michael Busselle/Robert Harding World Imagery), 134 (Christophe Boisvieux), 135 (Michael Busselle/Robert Harding World Imagery), 136–137 (Christophe Boisvieux), 138–139 (Doug Pearson/JAI), 140 (A/Philippe Lissac/Godong; B/Michael Busselle), 141 (Christophe Boisvieux), 142–143 (Altrendo Panoramic), 149 (Ethel Davies/Robert Harding World Imagery), 155 (Arthur Thévenart), 166 (Richard Klune), 170 (Arthur Thévenart), 178 (Catherine Karnow), 179 (Fridmar Damm/zefa), 184 (B/Owen Franken), 185 (Michael Busselle/Robert Harding World Imagery), 190 (T/Owen Franken; B/Paul Almasy), 191 (Frank Lukasseck)

2007 Barnes & Noble

ISBN-13: 978-0-7607-9116-5
ISBN-10: 0-7607-9116-3

Printed and bound in China

1 3 5 7 9 10 8 6 4 2

Page 1: The Tricolor flutters proudly in Arles.

Pages 2–3: Lavender around Sault in the Vaucluse.

Right: Bonifacio lies in the south of Corsica, separated by the Strait of Bonifacio from Sardinia. This is the nave of the cathedral in the citadel.

Contents

Introduction

By the end of the last ice age, around 450 B.C., the Celts had populated the country eventually to be named France, sweeping across the northern and eastern sides of the land. These fierce and strongly independent tribes, called the Gauls, left a mark on French culture and tradition that remains to this day. Still in the departments of Brittany and Normandy, the locals consider themselves Celtic foremost and French secondary. The Celtic roots in Brittany are even apparent in the local traditional costumes and music, even playing an instrument that appears very similar to a set of Scottish bagpipes.

To the South came the Greeks in 600 B.C. They founded the port of Massalia—later to become Marseilles. Life for the new people of France remained calm until 58 B.C. when Julius Caesar, bent on recognition and power through world domination, invaded. Despite a brave struggle from the Celts and their leader, Verçingétorix, the country was conquered in the name of Rome. Life under Roman rule was not all bad however. The invaders brought with them great architecture, roads, and waterways and the small towns flourished into cities. The burgeoning town of Lutetia on the banks of the River Seine began to bloom and would later become the sprawling metropolis now known to the world as Paris.

Drawn by the new prosperity that the country was enjoying, many barbarian tribes crossed the border into France and made it their new home; these included the Franks, the Goths, the Burgundians, and the Vandals. However, it was this increased influx of peoples that would prove to be Rome's undoing. By 486 B.C. Roman rule in France was beginning to teeter and a Frankish king, Clovis I, defeated the Romans in battle and crowned himself the new King of "Francia."

Clovis' successors, unfortunately, were not as decisive and soon the throne had passed to the Carolingian Dynasty. Pepin the Short, the son of the great French hero, Charles Martel, who routed the Muslim hordes from France, seized power from the Frankish royals and ruled successfully alongside

BELOW: Southeast of Toulouse, the walled city of Carcassonne has been inhabited since the third millennium B.C. and was first fortified by Julius Caesar.

ABOVE: Physical map of France showing major towns, roads, and geographical features.

his wife, Big-Footed Bertha. The throne then passed to his son, Charlemagne, in A.D. 768 and remained with him until his death in A.D. 814. Charlemagne strengthened his position by creating a huge Frankish Empire, making himself the first ruler of a Western empire after the collapse of Rome. He created the Holy Roman Empire and doubled the size of his kingdom to include Germany and Italy. On his death the throne passed to his last surviving son, Louis the Pious but his legacy was not destined to survive longer than one generation. When Louis' two sons inherited the realm, it was split between them thus taking the initial step towards separate German and French states.

After much rivalry and in fighting between the many separate duchies throughout the country, the Count of Paris—Hugh Capet—succeeded to the throne and declared himself King of all France. Despite his territory being only Paris and some surrounding lands, his dynasty was to remain on the throne until the Revolution in 1789 where many of his progeny would meet with a swift and sharp demise.

During the Middle Ages, religious fervor swept the country and France built some of the finest

churches in the world, Mont Saint Michel, the Benedictine Abbey at Cluny (now destroyed), and Notre Dame in Paris are just a few examples. Yet the ability to work together to create a great country still eluded the aristocrats. Even with the advantage of powerful and wise monarchs such as Louis IX and Phillipe the Fair, the country was still torn apart by the constant wars between the many independent and often rival duchies. This was all to come to a head in 1337 with the beginning of the Hundred Years War against the English. With the support of Burgundy, the English attempted to capture France. The war could not have come at a more difficult time for the French. Plague swept through the nation between 1337 and 1350, and King Charles VI began a swift descent into lunacy in 1392 making diplomacy between the rival dukes impossible.

In 1415, English King Henry V led a momentous battle against the French at Agincourt and, despite being overwhelmingly outnumbered, won. When Charles VI finally died in 1422 the title of "King of France" was handed to Henry VI—the grandson of Henry V.

The morale of the French people seemed at an all time low until a fervent peasant girl, Joan of Arc (or Jeanne d'Arc), inspired by the voice of God, led a revolt against the English. She fought battles with fierce determination and was eventually successful in crowning Charles VII at Reims cathedral in 1429. Joan was later betrayed and sold to the English by Burgundy in 1431. In the town square in Rouen she was burned at the stake for the crime of heresy. Joan was just nineteen years old, yet her patriotic spirit spoke to the people of France and revived their fighting spirit. The struggle against the English started anew and much of the country was recaptured. The English were not completely ousted from France until 1558 when they were finally forced to leave Calais.

The arrival of the sixteenth century brought with it the Renaissance. Art and literature flourished, explorers traveled to America and the religious teachings of Luther and Calvin found new devotees amongst the French. All people, not just the aristocracy, were absorbing newfound knowledge. The rise in Protestantism led to a bloody religious war with the established Catholic state, which culminated in a terrible massacre on St. Bartholomew's Day in 1572. Thousands of Protestants were savagely cut down by royal troops while they were praying.

Just when things seemed to be at their darkest for the Protestants, a series of strange assassinations and deaths led to the crowning of the first protestant king. Henri IV, one of France's best-loved monarchs, was brought to the throne and won the citizens' hearts with his womanizing ways and general "joie de

ABOVE: France is an intoxicating mixture of the old and the new. This is Paris' famous Centre Georges Pompidou, built in the 1970s to the design of architects Renzo Piano, Richard Rogers, and Sue Rogers.

RIGHT: The beautiful Pont de Normandie opened on January 20, 1995, linking Le Havre to Honfleur across the River Seine, a length of over 7,000 feet.

PAGES 10–11: With a foreground of France's favorite windowbox geraniums, this photograph shows how the Cathedral of St.-Front dominates the skyline of Périgueux in Aquitaine. Built between 1125 and 1250 on the site of an earlier church, the cathedral was restored in the nineteenth century by Paul Abadie, a local architect who would go on to win the competition to design Sacré-Coeur in Paris.

90

vivre." He converted to Catholicism to quiet the fears of the populace, declaring, "Paris is worth a Mass." He also granted religious tolerance to the Protestants under the Edict of Nantes in 1598. Not everyone was happy under Henri V's peaceful regime and a religious fanatic stabbed him to death in 1610. The whole country mourned his loss.

His successor, Louis XIII, was still very young when handed the crown but his Machiavellian advisor, Cardinal Richelieu, was immediately on hand to advise him. Under Richelieu's guidance Louis XIII invested further in France's North American assets and founded the Academie Française in 1653, but everything was not so rosy for the French people. As so often happens in the world of political intrigue, it was the masses who suffered—and "intrigue" was Richelieu's middle name. His costly and questionable Thirty Years War against Emperor Ferdinand left the people in poverty and starvation because in order to pay the military costs he had initiated new and crippling taxes. This caused considerable conflict between his personally installed tax collectors and the peasants. There were many uprisings that Richelieu dealt with harshly. Fear kept the people in line and Richelieu even reneged against the Edict of Nantes by laying siege to the Protestant city of La Rochelle. He died in 1642 and was followed by the king a year later, leaving the monarch's five-year-old son Louis XIV on the throne.

The reign of Louis XIV was the longest of any European monarch—seventy-two years—and he increased France's power through conquest. Despite a definitive triumph against the Spanish Army at Rocroi in 1643, unrest amongst the French people was rife. This dissatisfaction was known as the "Fronde" and developed into the Franco-Spanish War in 1648 when Spain saw an opportunity to aid the rebels and have revenge at the same time. Eventually, the Spanish again were crushed in defeat and the cost for meddling in France's affairs was high. Under the Treaty of the Pyrennees, signed in 1860, France took northern Catalonia.

Despite these conflicts, the reign of Louis XIV—known also as the Sun King—is recognized as the pinnacle of French monarchy. Eager to be remembered as a man of culture and a sponsor of the arts, Louis invited many famous artists and writers to court and he encouraged Jean-Baptiste Lully to set up the French Opera. Architecture was also important to the king and Jules Hardouin Mansart—now made immortal by his immediately recognizable Mansard-style roof—became France's foremost architect.

Unfortunately, perhaps the most enduring memory attached to the Sun King was his ability to spend

ABOVE: Paris is a country of restaurants and bars—perhaps because of this it is the most visited country in the world, with over 79 million foreign tourists annually.

LEFT: Burgundy is known the world over for its wines and food—its capital, Dijon, gives its name to a classic French mustard.

Cheese

France's second most popular export, cheese, has reached new heights of gastronomic excellence. The French produce more than 450 different types of cheeses, including cheese made with cow's milk, goat's milk or ewe's milk (the world famous Roquefort, for example). Of the many kinds made, only 35 carry the highly prized *Appellation d'Origine Controlée* (AOC) certificate, meaning the cheese has been manufactured according to ancient traditions and was made in a particular region of France.

Many cheeses are inextricably linked to the departments of their origin. For example, most French people immediately associate like creamy taste of Camembert with Normandy, the strong and tangy aroma of Cantal with the Auvergne or the slightly sweet, nutty flavor of Comté with the Franche-Comté area.

Many of France's better-known cheeses have been produced for hundreds of years with only slight changes to the recipes. Camembert is thought to have been around since the seventeenth century although the monks who made it had been experimenting with various formulas since the eleventh century. The legend of how the winning technique was finally found begins with the accredited inventor of Camembert, Marie Herel, being given the secret to making soft cheese by an abbot who was fleeing the anti-religious fervor of the Revolution. The rest is history. Camembert remains one of France's most popular cheeses, both home and abroad, and Normandy produces 15,000 tons of the famous cheese *every* year.

Known as the "King of Cheeses," Roquefort is one of France's noblest and therefore most expensive cheeses. King Charles VI gave the villagers of Roquefort the exclusive manufacturing rights in 1407 and during the seventeenth century the Parliament in Toulouse severely punished anyone daring to use the Roquefort name illegally. The rich blue-green veins in Roquefort are actually the spores of microscopic mushrooms that are cultivated on unleavened bread. The cheese is then left to age in natural caves in the mountains. The cool air promotes the bacteria, *Penicillium roqueforti*, to work its way through the pale curd.

Above: The Mémorial des Martyrs de la Déportation remembers the 200,000 deported from France by the Nazis. The courtyard sculpture represents the imprisonment and torture of those deported during the Nazi era.

the country's money. The luxury of the Palace of Versailles is legendary and it took thirty thousand workers years of labor to build it. It was big enough to house the entire court, which consisted of roughly six thousand people. Louis claimed to hate Paris and wished to make Versailles his new base. His plan in building such an ostentatious and opulent palace was that the aristocracy would be ever-present and somewhat dependent on him and therefore more submissive. He was right. Nobles vied for a place at court and would do anything to be allowed into his inner circle. It is rumored that the nobility were treated as little more than servants at Versailles. This did not seem to bother them as they fought for positions such as "holder of the king's shirt" or being the person who could shout, "The king's meat!" when it arrived at the dining table. Louis also chose his ministers from the lesser nobles and the bourgeoisie, thus keeping the aristocracy out of positions of power and free from any ambitions directed towards the throne.

Thanks to Louis' many wars against the Spanish and Dutch, France's territory grew and its army was the largest in Europe. The expense of this perpetual conflict took its toll on the lives of the common people, with whom Louis had now completely lost touch. Surrounded by luxury, he saw nothing of the poverty that gripped his people and discontent began to bubble into anger. Louis also went on to revoke the Edict of Nantes and ordered the destruction of any Protestant schools and churches. Many Protestants fled the country in fear of their lives, including two hundred thousand artisans that France badly needed.

The Sun King died in 1715 of gangrene, leaving his grandson, five-year-old Louis XV, in power. In spite of a mediocre reign that lasted until 1774, France under the new king gained a reputation as the most sophisticated and enlightened country in Europe. However Louis XV did not inherit any of his grandfather's military acumen. Although he managed

to annex Lorraine into France's borders following his defeat of the Austrian empire in 1738, he also lost all of France's North American empire following the Seven Year's War (known as the French and Indian Wars in the American theater) against England. All lands fell to the victor under the signing of the Treaty of Paris in 1763. Nonetheless, the kingdom was enriched by the purchase of Corsica from the Genoese in 1768.

Louis XV died of smallpox at Versailles in 1774. Because his son had died nine years earlier, the crown passed to his grandson, who became King Louis XVI at the age of nineteen.

During the American Revolution, France saw a perfect opportunity for revenge against Britain and supported the American rebels in their quest for autonomy. The next time the Treaty of Paris was signed in 1783, it was Britain that had to give up some of its claims in North America. Victory was a double-edged sword for the French monarchy, because the importance of the Americans revolutionary stance against an oppressive and greedy monarchy soaked into the French people's collective consciousness. Many renowned thinkers stoked the flames with their theories. Montesqueiu put forward an argument for political reform, Rousseau urged for monumental changes in education and society, and Voltaire lampooned oppression on all fronts. This change-oriented mindset was fueled by the increased taxation of the populace to cover the massive military expenses of the American campaigns and led to the French Revolution—which was to change the face of the country forever.

On the night of July 14, 1789, a mob of angry Parisians laid siege to the Bastille prison, killing the governor and many guards in the process. Spurred on by the bravery and audacity of the rebels, peasants across the country organized themselves into the National Assembly and stripped the nobility and the clergy of their privileges. Rather than individual provinces, the country was organized into 83 departments, the Tricolore became the national flag and the *La Marseillaise* was adopted as the new national anthem.

BELOW: Cannon outside Les Invalides in Paris. The military history of France is on view in the musuems and monuments (including the tomb of Napoleon) in Les Invalides. These cannon at the northern gate were taken in the mid nineteenth century after the Bombardment of Shimonoseki in Japan.

BELOW: The Loire Valley is renowned for its many beautiful chateaux—none more wonderful than Chenonceaux, built by King Francis I for his mistress Anne de Pisseleu, duchess of Etampes.

Unbeknown to the newly formed Republic, Queen Marie-Antoinette had called for aid from her brother, the Emperor of Austria and he quickly declared war. Counter-revolutionary action in northern France threatened the stability of the new regime even further. The First Republic took an offensive position and abolished all royal authority. Louis and his family were arrested while trying to escape France and sentenced to death as enemies of the state. Louis XVI met his end on the guillotine on January 21, 1793, in the Place de la Concorde in Paris.

The following years were not a good period in France's history. Paranoia and fear ruled and under the leadership of Citizen Maximilien Robespierre more than 40,000 people were put to death for opposing or even voicing concern over the authority the Republic wielded. This period became known as "The Terror," where ordinary people were too afraid to speak out against the atrocities happening every day in the name of France. It lasted four years and even claimed the life of Robespierre in 1794.

Salvation for France came in the form of a young Corsican general named Napoleon Bonaparte. The confusion and lackluster leadership that followed the four-year Reign of Terror was the ideal time for an ambitious man to seize control, which Napoleon did in 1799. He strengthened his hold on France by initiating the Code Napoleon, a body of civil legislation that remains the cornerstone of the French legal system even today. He also reorganized the monetary and education systems and established the first Bank of France. Through careful legislation and strong leadership he managed to unite a country divided by wealth, status, and even birthplace. He was crowned Emperor of France in Notre Dame de Paris in 1804.

Napoleon's success in battle led France into the age of a mighty empire, but it was his insatiable thirst for power and conquest that would prove to be Napoleon's downfall. Napoleon's many successes in war spurred him on to yet more battles, including some that were ill advised. He also erected many monuments to commemorate his prowess, including

the world famous Arc de Triomphe in central Paris, which depicts some of his finest victories. His disastrous expedition into Russia and his many subsequent defeats led to his loss of the throne and he was banished to the small island of Elba.

Napoleon remained confined on the island until 1815, when idealistic and loyal sympathizers to the Emperor expedited his return to power. In a daring coup, Napoleon once again took the throne for period that is now referred to as the "Hundred Days." Following his ignominious defeat at Waterloo, Napoleon was once again exiled—only this time to the more remote island of St Helena in the Atlantic Ocean, where he was kept under British supervision.

Lost for a leader, the French monarchy was restored. King Louis XVIII was crowned as the next king of France and began a period of repair known as the Restoration. The fervor of the Revolution had led to some extensive damage of both churches and chateaux; this was his attempt to reverse some of that destruction. However the people were not glad to be in the service of a bloated monarch once again after the freedom and increase in status the Revolution had offered. The status quo went into sharp decline following Charles X's injudicious decision to restrict the freedom of the press. The ensuing riots lasted for three days and the situation became so dangerous that the king fled Paris. He was replaced by his cousin, Louis-Phillipe, who claimed to have republican sensibilities.

In many ways the following years were extremely productive. Towns and cities grew, railways flourished and transformed the capital city, photography was invented by Louis Niepe in 1816, and historic literature became a respected art form through the works of writers such as Alexis de Tocqueville and Jules Michelet. Despite all this, the reign of Louis-Phillippe was also destined to fail. Unfair voting laws and the banning of an anti-government feast in Paris led to his abdication and the beginning of the Second Republic.

A presidential election was called and the victor was Louis Napoleon, nephew of the previous emperor. Following his success and faced with a largely monarchist parliament who saw his rule as a temporary stopgap until the restoration of a king, he staged a coup, arrested his opponents in the election and declared himself Emperor of France in 1851. The country was once again under the rule of a tyrant.

The new Emperor Napoleon III (Napoleon Bonaparte's son had briefly reigned as Napoleon II when the elder abdicated after his defeat at Waterloo) continued in his uncle's illustrious footsteps and waged war in order to expand his empire. Savoy and Nice were taken from Italy and became part of France.

Wishing his capital city to be the envy of the world, Napoleon III commissioned Baron Georges-Eugène Haussmann to revitalize Paris. This innovative and daring man would change the face of the city, making it the grand metropolis we see today. He designed the Bois de Boulogne in the center of Paris; built new and wider streets, as well as sewers, schools, and public buildings such as libraries and opera houses; improved existing parks; and demolished hundreds of homes in order to create thousands more. Art and innovation continued to flourish during this period.

Unfortunately Napoleon III began an impossible war against Prussia—allegedly after the Prussian leader, Otto von Bismarck sent him a telegram making fun of his moustache. Defeat was inevitable and the Second Empire fell. Napoleon III was captured by the enemy army and France was forced to cede Alsace and Lorraine.

The Third Republic took over and things improved for France over the next seventy years.

Corsica

The sun-baked island of Corsica possesses a landscape of surprising disparity. Surrounded by more than 600 miles of breathtaking coastline, including two hundred sandy white beaches, the island also has vertiginous mountain ranges, sheer rock cliffs, shimmering mountain lakes, forests, orange groves, and olive plantations. There is even a small desert in the northern part of the island. Most of the countryside is covered in dense shrub and sweet-smelling flowers known locally as "maquis." The locals are an attractive mix of French hospitality and Italian hot-blooded passion.

Corsica has not always been included in the French territories. From the eleventh to the thirteenth century, the Italian state of Pisa ruled the island. In 1284, the enemy of Pisa—Genoa—captured Corsica and ousted the Pisans. Due to its proximity to Africa and vulnerability to coastal attacks, the Genoese built numerous watchtowers along the shoreline and citadels for protecting the populace, many of which survive today.

After so many years under foreign rule, the Corsicans rebelled in 1755 thanks to the inspiring leadership of Pasquale Paoli. They successfully ejected the Genoese and quickly established the most democratic political system in Europe for that era. The most Italian of customs—the blood vendetta—became illegal, schools and universities were opened, and the country agreed the new national emblem would be The Moors Head. Legend has it that the scarf tied across the Moor's head had originally been secured over his eyes like a blindfold, but the newly free Corsicans changed it into a head scarf to symbolize the newfound emanci pation of the people.

This liberation, unfortunately, was not permanent. Genoa gave up its rights to the island and sold Corsica to King Louis XV of France in 1768. The following year the Corsicans were crushed under the heels of the powerful French army. The island officially became part of France in 1769.

Although France's military and worldwide political importance had diminished to some extent, the French were still the envy of the world simply because of their natural exuberance and love of life. In fact it was around this period when Paris first began to evolve into a raunchy, untamed mistress of a city—an image that is retained today. One reason behind this exciting and intoxicating new aura surrounding the capital was the number of writers and artists who found their spiritual home in Paris. (Not to mention the copious amounts of absinthe and opium they consumed also made for an unpredictable and exhilarating atmosphere.) Paris hosted Universal Expositions in 1855, 1867, and 1889. The 1889 exposition is of course now legendary because it heralded the introduction of the Eiffel Tower. This carefree time ended abruptly in 1914 with the outbreak of World War I.

German troops found their way quickly into France but were met with immediate resistance from French and Allied forces. Lengthy trench warfare halted the Germans progression into France, but this kind of fighting took a terrible toll and the French people paid a high price for freedom. Nowadays every village in France, no matter how small, has a plaque listing all the names of its fallen soldiers. When the war finally ended in 1919, France regained Alsace-Lorraine through the Treaty of Versailles and was awarded a fortune in reparations.

Paris of the 1920s, having recovered quickly from the war, bounced back with considerable style and *laissez-faire*. Called *Les années folles*—the crazy years—Paris embraced its brazen, hedonistic image and champagne flowed like water. Not all of France was this carefree. The depression of the 1930s hit the masses hard and made France's political structure very unstable. The nearby Spanish Civil War stirred up anger among the French and the increased military force built up under Hitler and Mussolini threatened to tip the balance in Europe. Despite an emergency

RIGHT: France's second city, Lyon, lies on the banks of the River Rhône. Among Lyon's claim to fame: it is known worldwide for its silk and textiles; it is the international headquarters of Interpol; it has a reputation for being the capital of French gastronomy; and the autoroute du Soleil that passes nearby is the scene every summer of huge traffic jams for those heading for the Mediterranean coast from the north.

Châteaux

The French word *château* can be quite misleading because it does not only refer to a castle or a mansion house. There are several interpretations that should be clarified. A château is a large house built in the country that is (or has been in its past) occupied by nobility. (The metropolitan version of this would be called a *palais*.) Usually these country houses won't have fortifications—unlike an English castle—but when they do they are termed *château fort*. However, in wine growing country, it is also customary for the estate to award itself the honorary title of château, whether somewhere established such as the world famous and incredibly expensive Château Lafite-Rothschild or the new breeds of exceptional and increasingly admired wines such as Château Grand Pierre in the Duras area. Very few of the winemakers will live in actual palaces, but are more likely to be hard-working farmers.

The Loire Valley has an extraordinary number of *châteaux*, more than three hundred in this one area of France. Known as the "Garden of France," many of the nobility moved their homes here to remain close to the throne, as this area was once the setting for the French court. Some of the most impressive examples of French architecture can be found within this valley, including the stunning and almost oriental looking Château Chambord—the superlative French castle. Also worth seeing are Chateau Chenonceau, home to the King's mistresses; Château Villandry, famed for its gardens; and Château d'Usse, which looks as though it has come straight from the pages of a fairy tale.

meeting between Britain, France, and Hitler in Munich in 1938, Germany invaded Poland on September 3, 1939, and World War II commenced.

With the benefit of hindsight it is easy to see how Germany found it so easy to capture a country as vast as France. The French believed their country completely impenetrable thanks to the Maginot Line, a fortified wall running through Alsace and Lorraine. When Germany began its blitzkrieg campaign, bombing France from a comfortably safe distance in Belgium, the Maginot Line was rendered useless and the country was soon captured by the enemy and subjected to German occupation.

In the aftermath, a young French general, Charles de Gaulle, headed straight for London to create a resistance movement. Meanwhile, occupying German soldiers basked in the champagne lifestyle of Paris, all the time executing resistance fighters, torturing civilians, and murdering one third of the French-Jew population in concentration camps. Following the successful D-Day campaigns in Normandy beginning in June 1944 and increasing Allied pressure on Germany, the end of the war seemed imminent and Paris' liberation inevitable. Hitler, never one to give in gracefully, ordered the entire city destroyed. His right-hand man in Paris, General Dietrich von Choltitz, could not bring himself to carry out the order. This hesitation saved the city as we know it today and earned him a commendation from the French government. By the August 25, 1944, Charles de Gaulle was paraded down the streets of the capital to thunderous applause. France was again free.

After the destruction caused by the war, France found itself in a more untenable position than it had been in for decades. The United States and Russia were now the only two superpowers in the world and France's position on the world's political stage had diminished even further. The national morale had taken a nosedive and the fallout from the years of occupation and the shame of collaboration with the Nazis led to a short period of self-recrimination. Suspected collaborators were executed and these deaths numbered in the thousands. The Fourth Republic was already faltering.

Rescue came in the stately form of General Charles de Gaulle. Pulling France through the doldrums, he encouraged the nation to "marry the century" and embrace the future. He bullied the National Assembly of the postwar Fourth Republic to issue a new constitution and ushered in a stronger, more confident Fifth Republic.

France began a new period of recovery, towns were rebuilt, and damage was repaired. The country regained its reputation for intellectual and philosophical excellence, thanks to the writings of Sartre,

Camus, and Simone de Beauvoir. Paris once again regained its title of the chic place to be and be seen.

Things took a turn for the worse again in May 1968. The youth of France, feeling constrained by the old-fashioned principles of their elders and the strict governmental control of the media, held demonstrations against the Vietnam War. These protests quickly descended into riots. Reminiscent of the riots that took place during the Revolution, students pulled up paving stones and barricaded themselves into the Latin Quarter of Paris. When others joined them (nothing bands the people together like

a good uprising), the government found it had a national emergency on its hands.

De Gaulle, realizing he was not perhaps the ideal man for this generation of French people, gave up his presidency and left political life. DeGaulle's prime minister, Georges Pompidou—who played a key role in resolving the student crisis—took his place as president, and the country enjoyed several relatively quiet and prosperous years under his leadership. Pompidou became ill with a rare cancer and died in 1974, but his name is immortalized in the famous cultural center in Paris.

In 1981, France elected its first socialist President, François Mitterand. He became the country's longest-serving president and remained in power until 1995. A visionary who instigated the *grand projets* of Paris, Mitterand wished Paris to be seen as a city of "architecture, sculpture, museums and gardens; a city open to imagination, ideas and youth." Regrettably many of Mitterand's final years in office were plagued with personal scandals and an unstable economy.

The presidency passed to right-wing Jacques Chirac, the former mayor of Paris, in 1995. By the

ABOVE: The Hôtel de Ville is Paris's city hall and can be found in the center of Paris, on the Rive Droite (the right bank of the Seine) just up from the Pont d'Arcole.

Wine

Perhaps the most popular and esteemed of this country's exports, wine from France is in a class of its own. One of the oldest wine-producing countries in Europe, the production dates back to 6 B.C. when the Romans introduced winemaking to the country. During the Middle Ages, vast vineyards grew up around monasteries where monks produced the all-important wine for mass. Their wine was considered far superior to any others.

Although the result of a complicated chemical process, the success of wine depends mainly on four separate factors: the type of grape, the climate, the *terroir*, and the skill of the winemaker. Terroir means soil but it refers to much more than that when associated with wine production. It encapsulates all the natural influences on the growth of the vines, such as underlying rock, altitude, angle of the land, and which way it faces. No two vineyards will have the same terroir and therefore no two vineyards can produce exactly the same wine.

Some winemakers still consistently outshine their competitors and become so skilled that the wine earns the title of *Grand Cru* (meaning "large growth"). Should this wine experience a year of ideal weather conditions then it will become a *Millésime*—a vintage. This is where France differs from New World winemakers. Because the French vintners are so susceptible to outside forces (for example, the INAO, the French bureau that awards AOC certification, will not allow them to water their vines should there be a drought) and as a result the wine differs from year to year, they have great vintages whereas the countries without these restrictions can produce the same wine year in year out.

There are countless winemaking regions in France, but the main ones are Alsace, Bordeaux, Burgundy, Champagne, Languedoc, the Loire, and the Rhône.

LEFT: France is one of the biggest—if not the biggest—producers of wine in the world.

Other French Dependencies

France has territories spread throughout the world, with differing levels of independence and population—some of the overseas French departments are uninhabited. Residents of all of the territories have a right to vote in French elections and each territory has a representative in Parliament. Overseas "departments" include Guadeloupe and Martinique, two islands situated in the eastern Caribbean; French Guiana, a territory on the northern coast of South America; and the Île de la Rénunion, a tiny island east of Madagasgar. France also has overseas "territories," which include a collection of volcanic islands in the southern part of the Indian Ocean, Adélie Land, which is part of the continent of Antarctica and also some far-flung islands in the Indian ocean.

Finally there are the "Overseas Collectivities," which still are counted as part of France's overseas territories, but tend to have much more autonomy. These include French Polynesia, which has its own president and assembly; Mayotte, an island in the Indian Ocean with an elected general council; Saint-Barthélemy and Saint-Martin, a collection of islands in the Lesser Antilles; Saint-Pierre and Miquelon, islands off the east coast of Canada; and Wallis and Futuna, situated in the Pacific Ocean. France also lays claim to the tiny Clipperton Island, a nine-square-kilometer coral atoll in the Pacific Ocean, roughly 800 miles southwest of Acapulco, Mexico. The island has no inhabitants and its only natural resource is tuna fishing.

dawning of the twenty-first century the economy had recovered, unemployment had dropped, and the controversial 35-hour workweek (a reduction from 39 hours) had been introduced. However, in keeping with fine French traditions, strikes and disputes remained a regular occurrence.

The recent 2007 presidential elections brought Nicolas Sarkozy—or Sarko as he is generally known—in to power. This right-wing leader advocates the scrapping of the 35-hour workweek and wants to bring France into the international markets and make people see that working hard is the only option for success. He is quoted as saying, "France has a tremendous advantage, a lot going for it, but I want to reunite France and the French people with success. In France, work does not pay enough. I want people to be compensated and respected for their work. I want people to understand the value of work."

Many hardened socialists fear that his plan for France's future is very similar to Margaret Thatcher's plan for the UK in the late twentieth century. It remains to be seen whether France can embrace the new millennium and become as united and as hard working as Sarkozy would like, while still retaining the cultural charms of its heritage and fascinating history.

Above: Lille in the north of France is a thriving town and a major point on France's rail network connecting the Eurostar link to Britain and Brussels with the French TGV network. Euralille is an urban remodeling project that began in 1991 and is now full of parks and modern buildings.

Right: A more traditional view of France as Le Cafe à Nuit in Arles prepares for lunchtime trade.

LE CAFE LA NUIT
Café la nuit

DEPARTMENTS OF FRANCE

After the destruction of the French Revolution, the new administration wished to eradicate everything that symbolized the old royalist ways of France. This included the division of lands. The old duchies of France were dismantled and the country was arranged into the more evenly balanced *départements.* The Constituent Assembly created these constituencies in 1790 by the Constituent Assembly to give the country a more logical structure and as a deliberate attempt to eradicate the cultural and class differences that existed between the provinces and thus create a truly egalitarian France.

Most of the newly created departments were named after the main rivers or geographical landmarks within them. The original number of departments was 83 but rose to 130 in 1810 following the many victories of Napoleon and the addition of lands

Pages 26–27: The old and the new—typical French urban architecture contrasts with Le Corbusier's stark Unité d'Habitation in Marseille. It is no wonder that Corbusier's Marseille architecture inspired the Brutalist style.

annexed into the French realm. Once Napoleon was defeated in 1814, the number fell again to 86. Following the addition of Nice and Savoy in 1860 and the creation of the Alpes-Maritime department from part of the Comte de Nice and the Var, the number rose again to 89. Alsace-Lorraine rejoined France as a result of Germany's defeat in World War I and the tiny area known as the "Territoire de Belfort" arrived in 1922. With the additional four overseas departments, the reorganization of the Parisian departments, and the division of Corsica, the quantity increased to 100.

The capital city of a department is called a *prefecture* or *chef-lieu de département.* The prefecture normally lies within the geographical center of the region. The original thought was that a man on horseback should be able to reach the periphery of the department within twenty-four hours, making the capital accessible to any local town in less than a day. Each department also has a *sous-prefecture*—a secondary capital and is administered by a general council, elected every six years.

Listed alphabetically, the departments are Ain, Aisne, Allier, Alpes de Haute Provence, Alpes-Maritimes, Ardeche, Ariège, Aube, Aude, Aveyron, Bas Rhin, Bouches du Rhône, Calvados, Cantal, Charente, Charente Maritime, Cher, Corrèze, Corse du Sud, Côte d'Or, Côtes d'Armor, Creuse, Deux Sèvres, Dordogne, Doubs, Drôme, Essone, Eure, Eure et Loire, Finistère, Gard, Gers, Gironde, Haut Rhin, Haute Corse, Haute Garonne, Haute Loire, Haute Marne, Haute Savoie, Haute Vienne, Haute Alpes, Haute Pyrénées, Hauts de Seine, Hérault, Ille et Vilaine, Indre, Indre et Loire, Isère, Jura, Landes, Loire, Loire Atlantique, Loire et Cher, Loiret, Lot, Lot et Garonne, Lozère, Maine et Loire, Manche, Marne, Mayenne, Meurthe et Moselle, Meuse, Morbihan, Moselle, Nivère, Nord, Oise, Paris, Pas de Calais, Puy de Dôme, Pyrénées Atlantiques, Pyrénées Orientales, Rhône, Saône et Loire, Saône, Sarthe, Savoie, Seine et Marne, Seine Maritime, Seine Saint Denis, Somme, Tarn, Tarn et Garonne, Territoire de Belfort, Val d'Oise, Val de Marne, Var, Vaucluse, Vendée, Vienne, Vosges, Yonne, and Yvelines.

LEFT: Bullfighting is popular in southern France where the great Roman amphitheaters of Arles and, here, Nîmes are the main centers.

Northern France

PAGES 30–31: The breathtaking view over Paris from the top of Notre Dame Cathedral. The Mansard windows that became so identified as Parisian are on almost every roof. Originally designed as a form of tax dodge—the French were taxed according to how many floors were beneath the roof—the style was revived during the rebuilding of Paris during the 1850s.

ABOVE: The Arc de Triomphe in central Paris was originally commissioned by Napoleon Bonaparte to commemorate his many victories in battle. It took thirty years to complete and unfortunately by that time Napoleon's losses far outweighed his victories.

RIGHT: Rouen Cathedral was built between 1201 and 1514, but due to extensive damage incurred during World War II it has recently undergone a thorough restoration. The cathedral is well known to lovers of Monet, who painted the gothic facade many times, apparently enthralled by the play of light across its structure.

ABOVE LEFT AND LEFT: Few sights in Paris are as immediately recognizable as the Eiffel Tower. Built for the 1889 World's Fair and designed by Gustave Eiffel, it was despised by Parisians when first erected—they nicknamed it "the Metal Asparagus." Due to be torn down in 1909, the tower was only saved from destruction when broadcasters realized its potential as a radio antenna.

ABOVE: The Hotel de Ville (French for City Hall) has been the home of the city administration of Paris since 1357. The existing building was built in the sixteenth century and had wings added to it in 1835. Gutted by fire during the Franco-Prussian War of 1871, it was rebuilt with an identical exterior and remodeled interior.

RIGHT: The magnificent cathedral of Notre Dame in Paris is a paragon of French Gothic architecture and has been the first church of French Catholicism for seven hundred years.

BOTTOM RIGHT: The old and the new stand together at the Louvre Museum and complement each other to dramatic effect. The Louvre was built in the thirteenth century as a fortress, then later became a royal residence. Not until after the French Revolution did it become a museum. Outside the main entrance to the Louvre is the impressive 70-foot-high Grande Pyramide, designed by American architect I. M. Pei.

BELOW: Construction of the Basilique du Sacré Coeur situated on the pinnacle of Montmartre Hill in Paris was initiated in 1873 and paid for by donations from penitent French Catholics after the disastrous Franco-Prussian War. It was finally consecrated in 1919.

PAGE 38: La Grande Arche de La Défense on the outskirts of Paris is one of many contemporary and awesome constructions. The arch was finished on July 14, 1989, and visitors can ride an elevator to the 35th floor to take in views across Paris and enjoy the modern art housed within.

PAGE 39: Metropolitan Paris as seen from the Eiffel Tower. Rising above the Paris rooftops is the shining dome of the Hotel des Invalides. Built in the seventeenth century by King Louis XIV to supply housing for injured war veterans, it played a pivotal role in French history when incensed Parisians broke in and stole weapons from the old soldiers on their way to storm the Bastille—thus beginning the Revolution.

PAVILLON SULLY

LEFT: The elegant city of Rouen in Normandy clings to the side of the meandering River Seine. Although now much of Rouen's medieval center has been lovingly restored, throughout history this city has been razed several times, either by plague, fire, or war. The central square of Rouen was also the site of Joan of Arc's trial and subsequent burning at the stake in 1431.

PAGES 42–43: The beautiful coastline along Calais' Côte d'Opale boasts many breathtaking views across the sea. The Cap Blanc Nez was once a cape, but sea erosion transformed it into a towering sheer cliff.

Above: Twilight falls across a sleepy town in Normandy. The canal winds its way through the quaint houses that hug the side of the waterway.

Right: The arches inside Amiens' gothic cathedral rise up to nearly 140 feet high and the cathedral building is the largest in France at 475 feet long. It was originally built in 1220 to house the head of John the Baptist.

Right: The River Somme winds through Amiens' cosmopolitan textile district, overlooked by the lofty cathedral spires. Once a busy industrial area, this part of Amiens is now a fashionable and busy bistro spot.

Pages 48–49: The church of Notre Dame in Calais is the only English-style basilica of its kind in France. It is the product of the extensive occupation by the English during the Hundred Years War. Now the building stands at the center of a huge cemetery dedicated to those lost in World War II.

GREPINET LOUIS
MORT POUR LA FRANCE le

Above: The tranquil gardens behind Notre Dame Cathedral on Paris' Île de la Cité provide a peaceful haven for visitors, away from the bustling metropolis that surrounds it.

Above right: The gardens of the Palace of Versailles were designed by André Le Nôtre. He drained marshlands, flattened hills, and even repositioned forests to create the perfect environment for the ornamental gardens, fountains and ponds.

Right: The chalk cliffs of Normandy known as "Les Falaises" stretch along the coastline. The Falaise d'Aval (pictured here) is famed for its impressive rocky archway. It is said to look remarkably like an elephant dropping its trunk into the sea.

LEFT: The splendid Chateau de Versailles was built by Louis XIV during the seventeenth century. Its regal opulence almost bankrupted the entire country yet it remains today one of the finest examples of French architecture and a testament to the "Sun King's" desire for self-glorification.

PAGE 54: The Chamber of Commerce in Lille was built in 1906 in a Neo-Flemish style. It stands not far from the delightful "Old Town" of Lille, a meandering set of medieval streets and squares filled with cafés, bistros, and bars.

PAGE 55: The gardens at Giverny, Normandy, are instantly recognizable to all fans of Monet. Bought by the painter in 1895 and subsequently transformed into the famed lily garden, it was the subject of many of Monet's final works.

Above: Just one example of the extremely fine and detailed sculptures found in and around the cathedral at Amiens.

Right: Originally a small chapel on the summit of the island, Mont Saint Michel has undergone many changes during its checkered history. It has been a monastery, a school, a fortress, and a prison. It was also the only part of northern France that held out against the English invaders during the Hundred Years War. It was declared a World Heritage Site in 1979.

Northwestern France

PAGES 58–59: Now known throughout the world for its eponymous liquor, the countryside in the Cognac region of Poitou-Charentes is striped by lush vineyards. The twenty-square-mile area where cognac is grown and distilled is known as "the golden circle" because of the luminous and clear sunlight that encompasses the landscape.

ABOVE: Construction of the imposing Chateau d'Angers in the Loire Valley began in 1230 and remained a seat of power throughout the medieval age. During the Hundred Years War against the English, it was a safe haven and was never sieged. The seventeen towers that surround the structure were not completed until 1240.

RIGHT: The monolithic, or underground, church at Aubeterre-sur-Dronne is carved completely out of the cliff on which it sits. The Church of Saint Jean can be reached by a hand-carved staircase and the main nave (pictured) is 65 feet high. To the south of the nave is a room containing more than eighty well-preserved sarcophagi.

LEFT: The beautifully preserved thirteenth-century walled town of Dinan on the River Rance is a magical and welcoming place. The quaint medieval streets are lined with small private cafés, bars, and family-owned bakeries, butcher shops, and artisan outlets.

PAGES 64–65: A ruined castle sits on the coast of the distant island of Yeu. It was built in the fourteenth century by Olivier de Clisson to protect the islanders from foreign invaders. It was declared a historical monument in 1890.

Left: Each year the grounds of the Chateau de Lathan hold a hunting fest. To the French, the hunt or "chasse" is a way of life and throughout the country successful hunters give chasse dinners to local villagers where the spoils of the hunt are eaten.

Above left: Just one of France's two hundred snail farms is here in the Pays-de-la-Loire. Inextricably linked with the idea of typical French cuisine, the snail was a staple food for Catholics during Lent. Nowadays, due to overharvesting and insecticides, most snails seen on the plates in France's restaurants have been imported from Greece or Turkey.

Above: The Chateau of Saumur on the Loire River was constructed in the tenth century by the Count of Blois but then later passed to the Count of Anjou who began rebuilding the round towers into a polygonal shape. During Napoleon's time the castle was transformed into a prison. Nowadays it is owned by the city and is undergoing extensive renovations in an attempt to halt its decay.

D 7
5 RIVARENNES
15 AZAY-LE-RIDEAU
21 VILLANDRY

HUISMES 6
CHINON 13
AVOINE 12
BOURGUEIL 16
L'INDRE

Pages 68–69: Chateau d'Ussé in the Indre-et-Loire department was the inspiration for Charles Perrault's *Sleeping Beauty*. Although nowadays it is a private residence, some parts are still open to the public.

Above: The quaint harbor in Roscoff, Brittany, is surrounded by sixteenth-century granite houses that cluster around the small bay. Although a cross-channel ferry port linking the town to England and Ireland, Roscoff has retained its quiet charm. The proximity of the Île-de-Batz means it is protected from some of the extreme winds that other ports in the area have to endure.

Right: Standing outside the picturesque village of Turquant in the Maine et Loire region of France is one of the last remaining windmills of Anjou. This one is located in the vineyard of La Herpiniere and was originally built in the fifteenth century but restored in 1972.

t de Fruits de mer
BAR
STATIONNEMENT
REGLEMENTE

Pages 72–73: A closer look at the old port in Dinan and the medieval buildings lining the street. Sidewalk cafés cover the length of the "Vieux Port" as visitors to this part of town often need to stop and rest after the extremely steep walk down from the main part of town.

Right: Just outside Poitiers is the glistening structure of the Parc du Futuroscope. A theme park with impressive 3-D cinemas based on multimedia using the cinematic techniques of the future. Some of the shows available are completely unique and not available anywhere else in the world.

Opposite, above: Hot-air balloons drift across the sweeping plains of the Loire River as it winds its way through the countryside of the Pays-de-la-Loire.

Opposite, below: The imposing Romanesque abbey of Saint Savin sur Gartempe in the Vienne department towers above the sleepy village below. The abbey is a World Heritage Site due to the many impressive and remarkably well-preserved murals inside.

Pages 76–77: The sleepy fishing town of Douarnenez on the coast of Brittany is a popular place for visitors.

BAR LE NEPTUNE
BAR

RESTAURANT DE LA RADE

Page 78: The interior nave of the church at Saint Savin is an imposing and impressive sight. The murals covering the ceiling date back to the eleventh century and depict the main stories from the Bible.

Page 79: This ruined watermill stands outside the stunning village of Angles-sur-Anglin, voted one of the most beautiful places in France. The village contains some sculptures dating as far back as fourteen thousand years and a magnificent chateau from the eleventh century.

Right: Sitting on the banks of the River Loire, the thriving city of Nantes has always been ahead of its time. Thanks to the slave trade it became one of France's busiest ports in the eighteenth century. With the abolition act of the nineteenth century it transformed itself into an industrial hub and embraced ship-building and the world's first public transportation system began here in 1826. Nowadays it is a youthful student town with half of the population under forty.

Le Shakespeare

Left: The entrance to the Vieux Port in La Rochelle, Poitou-Charentes, is protected by three huge white towers. Built from the local limestone during the 1600s, these monuments have earned the town the nickname of "La Ville Blanche" (The White Town) because of the way they catch and reflect the light of the sun until seeming to glow.

Left: The town hall building in the pretty town of Pouliguen in the Loire-Atlantique. This popular seaside resort has only five thousand inhabitants but during the summer months the population inflates to forty thousand.

Right: The attractive seaside town of Palmpol along the Côtes d'Amour in Brittany is an ideal place to enjoy the fruits of the sea. Oysters are a local specialty here and are served fresh from the sea in many of the local seafront restaurants.

Below: The fortified town of Villebois-Lavalette is built on a hill and dates as far back as Roman times, although initially it was just a Gallo-Roman villa close to the main road that joined Périgueux to Saintes. By the thirteenth century it had become an impressive castle with seven towers. Even Louis XIV stayed here and turned it from a fortress into a more opulent home. Unfortunately much of it was destroyed during the Revolution and only a few scattered towers remain.

Central France

PAGES 86–87: The picturesque commune of Vezelay in Burgundy is noted for the Basilica of Saint Magdalene that has stood high above the village since its construction during the ninth century. Legend has it that the bones of Mary Magdelene were brought to the town by a monk named Baudillon at the end of the first millennium. Following the pope's confirmation of authenticity, Vezelay has been a popular stop for pilgrims.

ABOVE: The village of Semur-en-Auxois in the Côte d'Or region stands on an outcrop of pink granite and is surrounded by the River Armancon. The heart of the town retains much of its medieval charm with many houses and buildings restored to their former glory.

RIGHT: Founded in 1118, the Abbaye de Fontenay nestles in a quiet wooded valley in the Burgundy region. It prospered throughout the twelfth and much of the thirteenth centuries, being named the Royal Abbey in 1269. Unfortunately the abbey was pillaged during the Hundred Years War and fell onto even harder times following the Revolution, when it was closed and became a paper mill. It has now been carefully restored and is a UNESCO World Heritage Site.

PAGES 90–91: La Rochepot is a tiny village situated on the "Route Des Grands Crus" in the Côte d'Or region of Burgundy. Named the gold coast because of the color the vine leaves change into during the dry summer months, this area is extremely popular with wine connoisseurs. La Rochepot is also famous for its remarkably well preserved thirteenth century castle that sits on a rocky peak high above the village.

RIGHT: The Loire Valley is often called the "Garden of France" and since the sixteenth century it has been a playground for royalty. Kings and nobility built numerous chateaux in this area in order to retreat from the pressures of life in Paris. There are now more than three hundred castles in this area, along with great architectural monuments and historic towns such as Angers, Orléans, and Tours.

PAGE 94: A closer look at the Chapelle St.-Michel d'Aiguilhe in Le Puy-en-Velay. The word *aiguilhe* means "needle" and refers to the tall, thin outcropping of rock on which the church is built.

PAGE 95: Situated in the entrance of a deep gorge stands the Chateau de Lavoûte-Polignac. Constructed during the thirteenth century and altered somewhat during the sixteenth and seventeenth centuries, the castle was a summer residence for the powerful Polignac family.

Left : The Abbaye de Fontenay was founded in 1118 by Saint Bernard of Clairvaux. After a tempestuous history and falling into ruin, it eventually became a paper mill owned by the Montgolfier family. Entrepreneur Édouard Aynard bought the abbey in 1905 and restored it to its former glory.

Above left: An interior view of Chartres cathedral. This impressive and historic building was one of the few to escape undamaged during the anti-religious fervor of the Revolution. The Revolutionary Committee decided to blow up the cathedral in a show of insurgent ire. It was saved by a local architect who pointed out the sheer volume of rubble the act would create and the years of cleanup—the committee changed its plans.

Above: The superbly Gothic cathedral at Chartres was constructed during the thirteenth century to replace a Romanesque cathedral that was destroyed during the huge fire of 1194 that consumed the church and most of the town. Miraculously, the church's most holy relic, the veil of Virgin Mary, escaped the fire and is now housed in a small chapel on the eastern side of the cathedral.

Page 98: The Reignac-sur-Indre region boasts many chateaux and palaces, and many of these contain the highly landscaped and geometric gardens so popular during the Renaissance. The Chateau de Reinac dating from the fifteenth century has a fine example of a circular maze.

Page 99: The striking town of Nuits-St.-Georges in the Côte d'Or region of Burgundy is a popular stop along the "Route des Grands Crus." Citeaux Abbey, founded in 1098, is located nearby and has greatly influenced the fate of the village, especially the local winemaking techniques.

Right: Chateau de Villandry in the Loire Valley is famed for its geometric gardens and flowerbeds that are in constant bloom between April and September. The gardens are laden with romantic imagery; for example, some represent love or music. The castle itself was finished in 1536 and was the last large Renaissance chateau to be built in the area.

LEFT: The Chardonnay grape harvest in the fields outside the picturesque village of Fulsse, in the Saone et Loire department of Burgundy. Wines from this area are highly prized.

PAGES 104–105: World War II took a significant toll on the people of France and nowhere is this more apparent than in the deserted village of Oradour-sur-Glane. Now a national monument, it has remained untouched since June 10, 1944, when the entire population was rounded up by SS troops and exterminated. Only six people escaped; 643 men, women, and children were massacred that day.

LEFT: The majestic ruin of a once-great tower overshadows the surrounding agricultural land in the Auvergne. France is scattered with historic monuments such as this, although many have survived the ravages of time a little better.

RIGHT: The amazing Art Deco Gare des Bénédictines in Limoges was constructed in 1929 and is one of the most impressive stations in France. The building is crowned with a huge dome of copper and the outside walls are decorated with intricate frescoes depicting typical rural scenes.

BELOW LEFT: The Chateau d'Anjony in the Cantal region of the Auvergne was built by Louis d'Anjony, one of Joan of Arc's master builders. He was instructed by Charles VII to build a keep that would protect the surrounding countryside. The keep still stands to this day and is a typical example of a fifteenth century fortress.

PAGES 108–109: The hospices in the lovely market town of Beaune were founded in 1442 by Nicolas Rolin, an advisor to the Duke of Burgundy. This charity runs hospitals for the disadvantaged and thanks to generous donations it now owns many vineyards in Burgundy.

ABOVE: The ostentatious Sainte Croix Cathedral in the city of Orléans was started in 1601 and underwent various additions and renovations all the way up to 1895, when the stained-glass windows were installed in the lower nave. These depict the life of Orléans' favorite adopted daughter (she was originally from Lorraine), Saint Joan of Arc.

RIGHT: The vineyards surrounding Pouilly-sur-Loire in the Nièvre department are world renowned for their white wines, called Pouilly Fumé. The word *fumé* in French means "smoked" and refers to the smoky taste these wines possess.

Right: Without doubt the superlative chateau in the entire region, Chambord is steeped in history, finery, and opulence that few can match, except perhaps Versailles. Chateau Chambord is now the largest castle in the Loire Valley but began life as a modest hunting lodge. King François I had it built into an enormous testament to his wealth and power. The chateau now sits within is own wildlife park covering 21 square miles and is enclosed by the longest wall in France.

Southwestern France

PAGES 114–115: Though dominated by the castle that looms above the village, Beynac-et-Cazenac is a magnificent place in its own right. There is evidence to suggest that people have settled here since 2000 B.C. and a reconstructed example of a prehistoric dwelling stands in the nearby archeological park. The castle was attacked by Richard the Lion Heart and changed hands many times during the Hundred Years War.

ABOVE: Bergerac, the town of Cyrano, also called the "Gateway to Perigord," is full of old buildings and ancient treasures. Here, leading toward the Rue Saint-Clar are some of the oldest houses in the town. They are made with cob, a mixture of mortar and straw, and have a corbelled upper level. The Tobacco Museum near here is housed in a private residence built in 1604 by a rich merchant family, the Peyrarédes.

RIGHT: Chateau de Hautefort in the Dordogne is a seventeenth-century castle famous for its English and French landscaped gardens. Perched high on a hilltop, it offers magnificent views over the Dordogne Valley. It also has a museum of medicine depicting life in a typical seventeenth-century hospital.

PAGE 118: Standing astride the mighty River Lot, Villeneuve-sur-Lot is a town of two separate and very different parts. The outer sections of the town are new, containing many malls and new housing and—unfortunately—very little soul. However, the central, older part of Villeneuve is full of medieval houses and buildings, particularly along the river's edge where ancient houses and terraces jut out into open air above the Lot.

PAGE 119: The popular village of Conques, hugging the sides of an untamed gorge, was declared an historical monument in 1838 and registered as a World Heritage Site. The village has for the past twelve centuries guarded a holy treasure inside the church of Saint Foy, a reliquary statue that receives more than 600,000 visitors every year.

RIGHT: Near the remote village of Montignac in the Dordogne are a complex series of limestone caves hewn from a cragged cliff face. The caves are called Lascaux and contain nearly two thousand Upper Pale-olithic drawings, dating them to approximately 15000–13000 B.C. They are mainly of bulls—as here—and other animals

Above: The medieval fortress of Chateau de Castelnaud perches high above the Dordogne River. It is mentioned in the history books from as far back as the thirteenth century during the troubled Albigensians Crusade—a vicious religious war against the Cathars. Fundamentalist Christians who believed theirs was the one true way, the Cathars were declared by the pope to be heretics and war began. The owner of the chateau in the 1200s, Bernard de Casnac, was a staunch defender of the Cathar faith and had the castle taken from him in 1214 and a garrison was established there. One year later, Bernard regained his castle and hanged the entire troop.

Above right: The town of Saint Émilion near Bordeaux is famous for the eponymous wine area in which it stands. There have been settlements here as far back as prehistoric times and vines have grown here since the Romans planted them in A.D. 2. The town takes it name from a hermit monk who settled here in the eighth century. The monks who followed him began the production of the famous red wine.

Right: One of the finest winemaking districts in the world, Bordeaux includes some of the planet's most celebrated vineyards; for example, both Mouton-Rothschild and Chateau Margaux are found here. The 444 square miles of vineyards in Bordeaux supply more than a quarter of France's wine stock, both red and white.

RESTAURANT

LEFT: Just one example of the two thousand cave paintings inside the caves at Lascaux. The caves were discovered in 1940 by four teenagers and became public after World War II. Unfortunately, by 1955 the sheer number of visitors and the carbon dioxide those visitors exhaled began to damage the paintings.

ABOVE LEFT: In the luxurious seaside resort of Biarritz stands the Hôtel du Palais. The resort was made popular and "exclusive" by Napoleon III and his Spanish wife, Eugenie, when they started using it as a regular summer retreat. The Hôtel du Palais was originally built for Empress Eugenie in 1854 as a summer residence but now operates as a lavish hotel.

ABOVE: The Vézère River streams from the Massif Central all the way to the Dordogne where it converges with the Dordogne River at Le Bugue. Apart from the world-renowned caves at Lascaux, the Vézère Valley contains 147 other prehistoric sites and settlements, earning the area the nickname "the cradle of mankind."

Pages 126–127: The breathtaking Lac d'Oredon in the Pyrenees covers an area of 113 acres and is found at an altitude of 6,066 feet above sea level. This beautiful and serene national park is a popular first port of call for many hikers attempting to climb higher into the surrounding mountains.

Right: One of the major beauty spots of the Lot valley is the village of Saint-Cirq Lapopie, perched on a cliff 300 feet above a winding river. During the Middle Ages, Saint-Cirq Lapopie was a major town and dominated by a fortress consisting of a number of castles and towers. Although now in ruins, the fortress still offers the best views of the area.

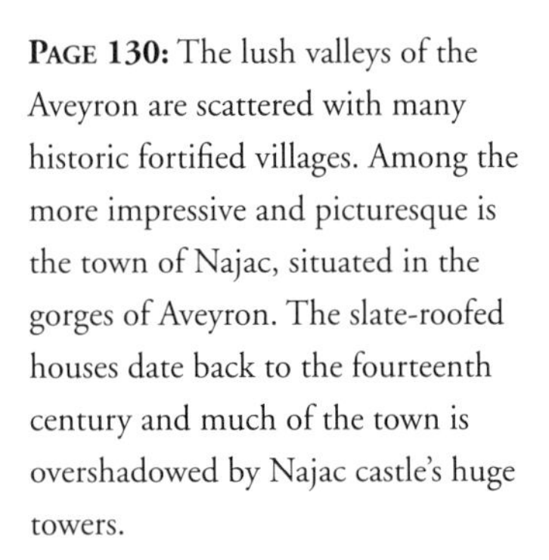

Page 130: The lush valleys of the Aveyron are scattered with many historic fortified villages. Among the more impressive and picturesque is the town of Najac, situated in the gorges of Aveyron. The slate-roofed houses date back to the fourteenth century and much of the town is overshadowed by Najac castle's huge towers.

Page 131: Following the appearance of the Virgin Mary to a 14-year-old peasant girl named Bernadette Soubirous in 1858, Lourdes became the world's most important Roman Catholic pilgrimage site. Five million people a year descend on the once-sleepy market town and more than half are invalids seeking a cure for their ailments. The Basilica of the Rosary is split into two levels, the crypt below is for silent prayer and the upper level holds the Basilique Superieur.

Above: Construction of the Valentré Bridge in Cahors began in 1308 and finished by 1378. It is the symbol of the town and has an interesting legend attached to it. Like many other bridges throughout Europe, it is known locally as the Devil's Bridge. The story begins with the Devil making a pact with a simple shepherd (sometimes an old lady) and agreeing to build the bridge in exchange for the soul of the first person who crosses it. The story inevitable ends with the Devil being outwitted and cast into the flowing river below.

Right: Close to the charming medieval town of Saint Céré stands the renaissance Chateau Montal. Although it fell into disrepair during the previous century, it was recently restored and fully furnished by a French oil billionaire and donated to the nation.

Page 134: In the heart of the ancient province of Quercy lies the peaceful village of Carlucet. It is noted for its picturesque countryside, waterfalls, and old stone-tower windmills.

Page 135: Near the charming village of Castelmau-Montratier stands this quaint church in the center of a lush and verdant vineyard. The nearby village is famous for its thirteenth-century country house and the three windmills that stand like sentries at the village entrance.

Right: One of the celebrated vintners in the Cahors region, Chateau de Lagrezette has won many medals for its richly flavored, dark (almost black) red wine.

Pages 138–139: The huge Dune du Pilat is the largest sand dune in Europe, stretching nearly two miles from the mouth of the Bassin d'Arcachon in Aquitaine. Studies have shown it is moving eastwards at a rate of almost 15 feet per year. It has consumed trees, a road, and even a hotel. There is currently a campsite on the end of the vast sand bank-although probably not for much longer.

LEFT: The church of Sainte-Foy in Conques was built in 1120 from the local limestone, giving the building its distinctive color. Thousands of visitors come to the town every year to visit the preserved skeleton of Sainte Foy, a martyr from the fourth century.

ABOVE LEFT: The serene and calming cloister inside the Abbaye La Romieu in the Gers department of France. The abbey was founded in 1062 by two monks who had returned from a pilgrimage to Rome.

ABOVE: Lining the cliffs above the River Alzou, the medieval site of Rocamadour is an unforgettable sight. Impossibly tall, thin houses cling to the sheer cliff face. Rocamadour has been a pilgrimage site since the twelfth century and obtains its name from Saint Amadour, whose remains are kept in a subterranean crypt hewn from the rock underneath the church of Saint Sauveur.

Southeastern France

CAPITAINERIE

Pages 142–143: Greek sailors founded the bustling port of Marseilles in 600 B.C. under the name Massilia, making it France's oldest city. The old terra-cotta colored port of Marseilles still survives and echoes some of the sultry energies from its nearby neighbor, North Africa.

Left: Inside the fortified walls of La Cité in Carcassone. After Carcassone was deemed superfluous by Napoleon when establishing a list of official fortifications, the walled city fell into complete disrepair and was almost demolished. It was only due to the insight and intervention of the local people that led to the employment of Eugène Viollet-le-Duc, famed architect and expert in restoration, who saved the town from ruin.

Right: The fortified town of Briançon in the Haute-Alpes has been an important military stronghold since the Roman occupation but it was the famed architect and military mastermind, Vauban, who surrounded the town with high walls and built a citadel.

Below right: Inside the calming enclosure of the Parc de Longchamps in Marseille stands this water tower, cleverly disguised as an ornamental fountain. The French are never ones to forsake aesthetics for the sake of practicality.

Pages 146–147: The terra-cotta, sun-baked village of Pigna stands on a hilltop looking out across the sea —a perfect place to stop and drink in the relaxed Mediterranean atmosphere and savor the local wines.

Page 148: A quiet coastal town, Porto in Corsica, sits serenely in a valley of eucalyptus groves on the edge of the Le Porto River. Surrounded by towering, red-hued mountains and close to the sprawling Réserve Naturelle de Scandola —a massive nature reserve containing sheer cliffs, grottos and unreachable coves—Porto seems like the last stand of civilization against an impenetrable and difficult landscape.

Page 149: Over two thousand years old and half in ruin, the Trophée des Alpes or the Trophy of Augustus is still an imposing monument. Originally built in 6 B.C. to commemorate the victories of Emperor Augustus in Gaul, it still dominates the town of La Turbie.

Right: Chateau de Quéribus in the Aude department was one of five castles built to protect the French border against the Spanish. It was also one of the last Cathar strongholds against the French army. Quéribus stands on the highest peak in its vicinity and is completely isolated, which allowed the retreating Cathars to simply slip out of the army's grasp and head for more sympathetic and tolerant countries.

Pages 152–153: Twelve miles east of Marseille lies the picturesque town of Cassis in the Bouches-du-Rhône. This area is popular because of its imposing cliffs and the breathtaking beauty of the "calanques"—a steep coastal gorge leading into the Mediterranean. Cassis also has a flourishing wine industry—pictured is the Sainte Magdeleine vineyard—and was one of the first vineyards to receive an AOC certificate.

LEFT: The gently sloping village of Zonza is situated within Corsica's interior mountainous region. The village sits at an elevation of nearly 2,500 feet above sea level and is close to the awesome rock formations of Col de Bavella.

ABOVE LEFT: An incredible feat of Roman engineering, the Pont du Gard is more than 160 feet high and it took one thousand men fifteen years to build. It was built to allow the aqueduct at Nimes to traverse the Gardon River.

ABOVE: The village of Villerouge-Termenès—surrounded by vineyards—of the Aude department in Languedoc-Roussillon boasts an excellently restored medieval castle at its heart. The castle now houses a restaurant and museum dedicated to the life of Guillaume Bélibaste—the last of the Cathars to be captured by the Inquisition. He was burned alive in this village in 1321.

LEFT: The Palais Longchamp was built in 1862 and marks the start of Longchamp Park in Marseilles. Four stone lions stand guard at the entrance and inside is a magnificent water tower, cunningly disguised as a decorative fountain. This building also houses the *Musée des Beaux Arts*.

Left: A colorful hilltop village looks out across the Alps in the Hautes-Alpes department. This was one of the first new *départements* to be created following the Revolution and this was also where Napoleon marched back into France after his exile in Elba.

Page 160–161: Being one of the highest towns in Europe naturally guarantees Briançon some of the most spectacular views across the mountains. The Alps stretch out across the horizon past the green valley below. Briançon has also been a very important military stronghold in past years as it protects the Col de Montgenevre, a critical mountain pass that leads directly into Italy.

LEFT: The amphitheatre in Arles dates back to the Roman occupation of the fourth century A.D. when Arles' importance grew and the city was often used as a military headquarters. This is one of the best examples of a well-preserved Roman theater in Europe and it is still used for bullfighting.

ABOVE: Out of Corsica's six awe-inspiring citadels, only this one at Corte does not stand on the coast. Built in 1419 at the confluence of the rivers Taviganu and Restonica by a Corsican aristocrat, the citadel's highest point is the chateau, known as the "eagle's nest."

PAGES 164–165: The arid limestone peaks of the Alpilles mountain range in Provence have been captured by many well-known painters, including Van Gogh. This barren area is home to many endangered species such as the Egyptian vulture and Bonelli's eagle.

Above: The Gulf of Porto on the western side of Corsica is well known for its ochre-colored rocks and clear blue waters. This, coupled with many inaccessible coves and bays, encourages a rich and varied selection of marine life.

Above right: Many myths and folk tales surround these standing stones in Corsica, but locals refer to this particular rock formation as "La Forge du Diable"—the Devil's Forge. Many similar megaliths surround the area and it is thought to be an ancient burial ground.

Right: The construction of Pont d'Avignon, also known as Pont St.-Bénézet, was inspired by the actions of a native shepherd who claimed angels had ordered him to build the bridge. The townsfolk made fun of him at first until he was miraculously able to lift a giant chunk of rock, thus proving his divine mandate.

LEFT: Corsica's 600-plus miles of mostly unspoiled coastline—including 200 white sandy beaches with azure blue seas—make it a popular tourist destination.

Eastern France

AUBERGE DU CHATEAU DE JOUX
PHARMACIE
LE FRAMBOURG

Pages 170–171: Standing on a hilltop overlooking the peaceful village of Cluse en Mijoux is Château Joux, believed to have been built by the Knights Templar in the eleventh century.

Above: Because of the area's ancient links with Rome, many fine examples of Roman architecture remain. This excellently preserved Roman amphitheater in the Rhône-Alps department is just one example of such antiquities.

Right: Named after the bishop who baptized King Clovis I along with three thousand Frankish soldiers, the Basilica of Saint-Remi in Reims dates back to the eleventh century and has been named a World Heritage Site.

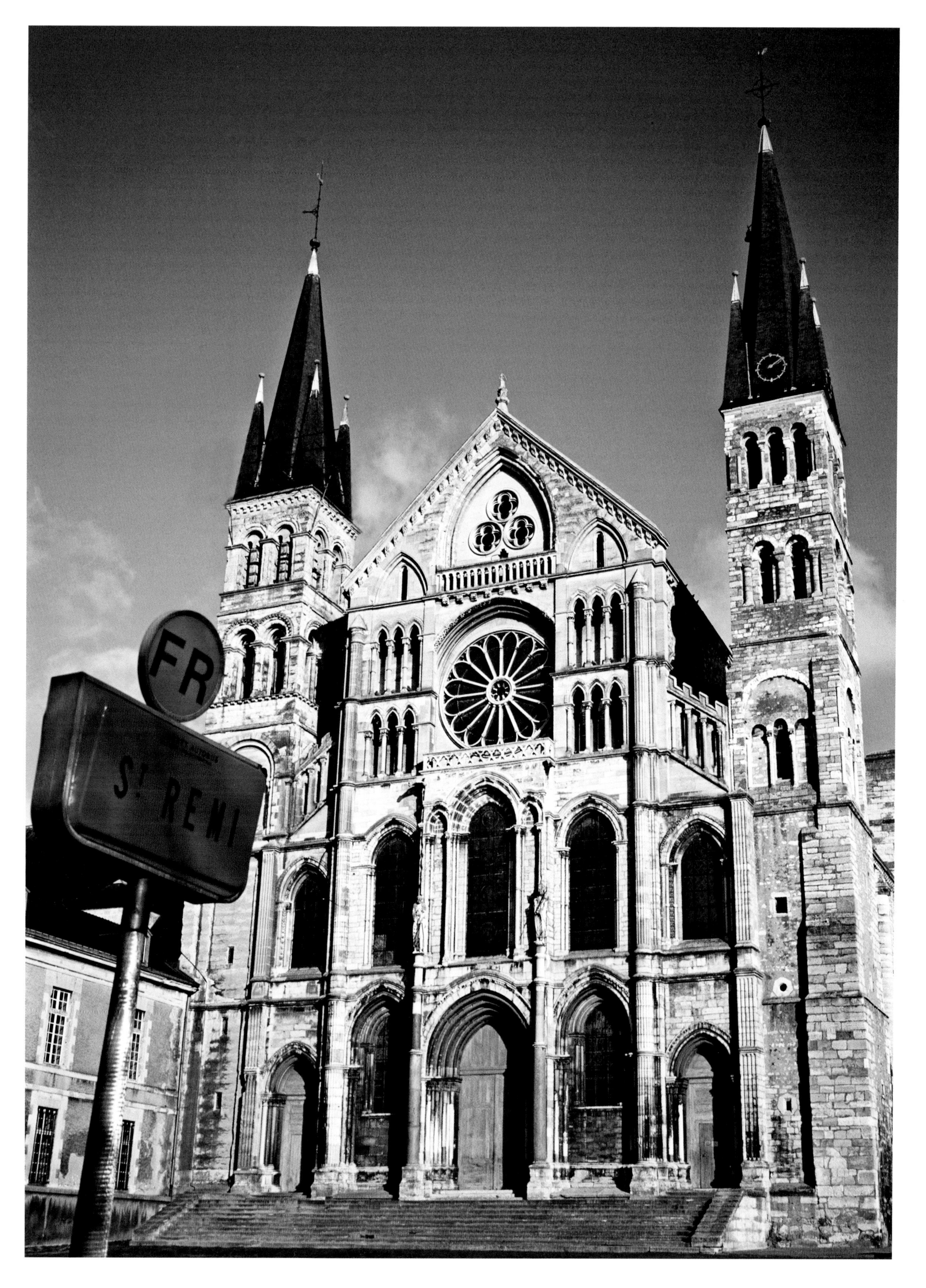
FR
St REMI

RESTAURANT
STANISLAS

Pages 174–175: Nancy was the former capital of the Dukes of Lorraine and still retains an opulent air. The Hotel de Ville and theater with its wrought-iron gates have been declared a World Heritage Site by UNESCO.

Right: Standing on top of the Basilica Notre Dame de Fourvière, an angel looks out across Lyon, known as the gourmet capital of France. The basilica was built in the late nineteenth century on the top of Lyon's "hill of prayer."

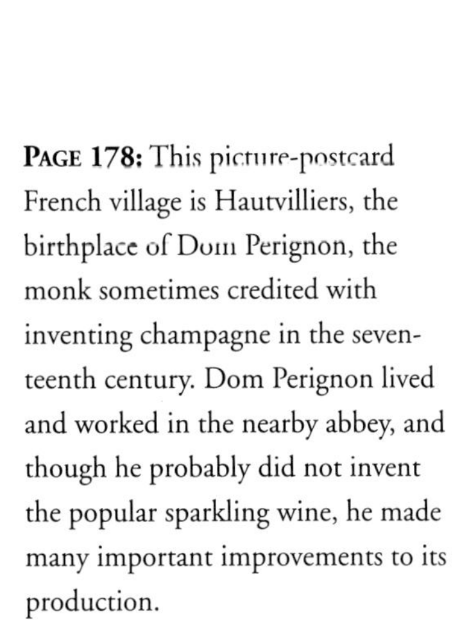

Page 178: This picture-postcard French village is Hautvilliers, the birthplace of Dom Perignon, the monk sometimes credited with inventing champagne in the seventeenth century. Dom Perignon lived and worked in the nearby abbey, and though he probably did not invent the popular sparkling wine, he made many important improvements to its production.

Page 179: One of the most attractive villages on the Route du Vin, Ribeauville is a charming eighteenth-century parish celebrated for its Grand Crus-Osterberg, Geisberg, and Kirchberg de Ribeauville.

LEFT: The gorges of the Ardeche offer unrivaled views of the surrounding countryside and many small villages such as this cling to the very edge of the precipice. The yellow-and-gray limestone cliffs are home to eagles and there are many secret caves to discover.

PAGES 182–183: The modern glass building that serves as home for the European Parliament in Strasbourg. There are other bases in Brussels, Luxembourg, Frankfurt, and The Hague. Many people see these buildings as a great symbol of the power a united Europe could achieve; unfortunately many more seem them as a large waste of money.

LEFT: Surrounding the famous town of Épinay are many champagne vineyards. Épinay is considered by wine connoisseurs to be the undisputed heart of the Champagne region.

ABOVE LEFT : The countryside of the Alsace is particularly noted for its undulating green hills and valleys covered in lush vegetation. Looking at the buildings in the village it is easy to observe the architectural influences of nearby Germany.

ABOVE: Lons le Saunier, the capital of the Jura department. The town is known for its wines and the refreshing saltwater spa that has been in operation here since the fifth century.

Pages 186–187: The Saline Royal or Royal Saltworks in Franche-Comte was built in the nineteenth century by Claude-Nicholas Ledoux and was originally constructed to be the model of an ideal city. Though never fulfilling its original purpose, it is now listed as a World Heritage Site.

Right: The charming "Petit France" area of Strasbourg is intersected by many canals. Numerous medieval half-timbered houses line the canals' edges.

Above: Steeped in grandeur and inspiring awe in all who see it, Mont Blanc is Europe's highest peak. Measuring 15,774 feet above sea level, it stands in the Alps—one of the most breathtaking mountain ranges in the world.

Right: The majestic mountains reflect on the still surface of the glassy mountain lake, Lac Blanc, near the popular ski-resort of Chamonix, not far from Mont Blanc.

Left: *The Lion of Belfort*, designed by Frederic Bartholdi (who also designed the Statue of Liberty) and completed in 1880. It was erected to celebrate the fighting spirit of Belfort that had held out for so long in the Franco-Prussian war of 1870–71. It is made from the local pink sandstone.